CW00686756

Just mercy

JOEL EDWARDS

Just mercy

JOEL EDWARDS

Copyright © Micah Challenge International 2010

Published 2010 by CWR, Waverley Abbey House, Waverley Lane, Farnham, Surrey GU9 8EP, UK.
Registered Charity No. 294387. Registered Limited Company No. 1990308.

The right of Joel Edwards to be identified as the author of this work has been asserted by him in accordance with the Copyright, Designs and Patents Act 1988.

All rights reserved. No part of this publication may be reproduced, stored in a retrieval system, or transmitted, in any form or by any means, electronic, mechanical, photocopying, recording or otherwise, without the prior permission in writing of CWR.

See back of book for list of National Distributors.

Quotes from *The Art of Compassion* by Compassion Art, on pages 24,25,39,40,53 are reproduced by permission of Hodder & Stoughton Limited (UK), and Faith Words (US).

Unless otherwise indicated, all Scripture references are from the Holy Bible: New International Version (NIV), copyright © 1973, 1978, 1984 by the International Bible Society.

Other versions used:
AV: The Authorised Version;
ESV: The Holy Bible, English Standard Version, published by HarperCollins © 2001 by Crossway Bibles, a division of Good News Publishers.

Concept development, editing, design and production by CWR

Printed in England by Nuffield Press

ISBN: 978-1-85345-557-5

Contents

Introduction

Very few Christians will ask you to leave the room if you talk about ministry to the poor. Even parts of the Christian Church that are nervous about social action have come to realise that you simply cannot separate love from action. So now, more than ever, thousands of churches are involved in acts of kindness.

There is another level of prophetic engagement, however, that is urgently needed. It is to be involved in biblical advocacy. In the words of Proverbs, it is to 'speak up for those who cannot speak for themselves' (Prov. 31:8). More often than not, though, it is to speak up *with* the poor who cannot speak up alone.

At the dawn of this millennium the world woke up to the notion that we have a moral responsibility to do something about extreme poverty – about the more than one billion people who live on less than a dollar each day. In response 189 nations made eight promises to the poor which were described as the Millennium Development Goals. These goals aim to halve extreme poverty by the year 2015.

Our study provides not a political but a biblical response to our promises to the poor. The work of Micah Challenge is a global Christian response to these promises, motivating Christians to bring Jesus into the equation. And in 2010 – when we are two-thirds of the way into making good our promises – we have an opportunity to do just that.

This study aims to open our eyes to our mission to the poor, and to motivate us to become involved in a global mission to the poor. This unique partnership between CWR, Micah Challenge and CompassionArt is all about remembering and responding to the poor. We are all grateful to Kingsway who have made available a selection of four songs from the *You Have Shown Us* CD as free downloads to help you reflect on the topic for each week.

Joel Edwards

Walking with God

Micah now and then

I know it was a long time ago, but in the UK during the 1960s *Catweazle* was a favourite TV programme. It followed the adventures of a medieval wizard who cast a spell and found himself in the twentieth century as a result. Every day for him was a culture shock, and his entire ability to survive was dependent on a young boy who protected, fed and helped him to find his way back to the past. Nothing Catweazle had to say seemed suited to the twentieth century.

I'm pretty sure Micah, too, would struggle today. But his message would be like a song in season. Fat-cat financiers made rich on the poor, sweat-shop owners and people pumped up with pride would all understand him clearly enough. And so would religious leaders!

We know relatively little about Micah apart from the fact that he came from a small town in the lowlands about twenty-two miles southwest of Jerusalem called Moresheth-gath and had a very clear sense of his own calling (Micah 3:8; 7:7). He was what scholars refer to as a 'minor prophet', whose main work took place between 742 and 687 years before Jesus was born. Micah, and other eighth-century prophets such as Amos and Hosea, lived at a time when the Jewish people were divided into two. The southern kingdom of Judah, which remained the religious centre as it housed the Temple in Jerusalem, was often at odds with Israel, which comprised the ten northern tribes, and is often referred to in the Bible as Samaria – the name of its capital city. But the prophets would frequently cross the political boundaries in order to take God's message to the divided people.

Micah's prophecies were aimed mainly at Jerusalem, where the religious observances associated with the Temple took place. This was a period of political alliances between neighbouring nations, and in this period Israel and Judah were very conscious of the neighbouring superpowers of Assyria and Egypt. The alliances made were usually aimed at securing financial and trading benefits.

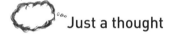 **Just a thought**

Micah is not giving a new answer, he is simply reminding them of the covenant law.

Mary Evans,
Bible teacher

When Micah appeared in Jerusalem, the people were enjoying a time of prosperity. But it was not prosperity with equality. The fat-cat landowners were getting rich at the expense of the poor and were straying from the commitment the people of Israel had made with God when they were founded as a covenant nation. Even more disturbing was that despite all the extortion and greed, the people thought that they could continue business as usual. Worship, in their minds, had nothing to do with their lifestyle outside the Temple. As far as they were concerned a lavish offering would make up for the more basic requirements of justice, mercy and kindness.

Micah would have been an uncomfortable presence for the people – not so much because his words were penetrating but because he was calling them back to what they already knew: that God wanted far more than religion. God wanted them to keep the promises which had shaped them as a nation (Exod. 20:1–17; Deut. 10:12).

Do have a look through Micah's entire prophecy. He begins with a warning of God's judgment to come (1:2–2:11), denounces the present leaders for being corrupt (3:1–12), presents a sense of the salvation which will follow despair (2:12–13; 4:1–5:15), and moves on to a powerful account of God's case against the nation (6:1–16), which includes the passage we will explore (6:6–8). What is also uplifting about this man is that in all of this he is also completely aware of God's hope. After judgment and challenge there is hope and redemption (7:8–20). And this is the spirit of the Scriptures. The message of the Bible is ultimately one of hope. God challenges us not just to make us feel bad about what we haven't done but to get us to change our ways and to make sure we don't miss out on hope.

Micah would have been at home at an Africa Aid concert like Jubilee 2000, or wearing his white armband in Make Poverty History. As far as he was concerned everything connected with worship involved doing justice and loving mercy. And this was made possible by a lifestyle of humility.

Watch your walk

I left Kingston, Jamaica for the UK aged eight. I returned for the first time when I was twenty-seven, and was very glad to be 'back home'. One day, though, as my wife and I were out for a walk someone shouted, 'Foreigner!' We had no idea who they meant. But they were addressing us. We thought we dressed and looked like Jamaicans. One simple difference, however, told everyone we were only visiting: it was the way we walked!

The Bible has quite a lot to say about 'walking'. In Genesis, for instance, Enoch, Noah, Abraham and Isaac are all described as men who walked with God (Gen. 5:22,24; 6:9; 17:1; 24:40; 48:15). It is one of the most natural things able-bodied people do. And, as far as Micah is concerned, in our walk with God three things should always mark us out from everyone else: we act justly, we love mercy, we flow with humility (Micah 6:8).

Working it out

What makes your 'walk' distinctive today, and how could you make it more so?

Just doing justly

Justice and the Disneyworld syndrome

Everyone should go to Disneyworld! Twenty years after my visit it still rates as one of my best experiences of all time – and I still have the Goofy photos to prove it! One of my many Disney memories is of standing in line for forty minutes waiting for a four-minute ride and hearing the same mechanical voice repeating, 'Please exit on the left-hand side. Please exit on the left-hand side ...' Why do I remember this? Because of the number of people who were coming off the ride on the *right-hand* side! Just four minutes of fun was enough to make them forget the words they knew by heart.

When it comes to justice most of us are in Disneyworld. After idolatry, God says more in the Bible about injustice than any other subject. But, even so, many of us who have attended church for decades can still count on our fingers and toes the number of Sunday sermons we have heard on justice. And this really does matter because what we preach and talk about affects what we do.

Is justice out of the question?

So what has made something which is so mainstream become so marginalised? It's probably because we have lots of questions about it.

Too political?

Well, for a start, justice is likely to end up being far too political for most of us. And there is no point denying it. No great movement for emancipation – from that of the Israelites in Egypt and the Jews in Babylon to the movements led by Wilberforce, Gandhi or Martin Luther King Jnr – is likely to avoid some degree of political involvement.

If you are neutral in situations of injustice, you have chosen the side of the oppressor.
Archbishop Desmond Tutu

Working it out

How do you react to this quote from Archbishop Tutu?

 **Just a thought**

In our time God's yes to the world reveals itself, to a large extent, in the church's missionary engagement in respect of the realities of injustice, oppression, poverty, discrimination and violence.
David Bosch,
Transforming Mission

Let justice roll down like waters, and righteousness like an ever-flowing stream.
Amos 5:24, ESV

Is justice the gospel?

This is an odd question because the Bible makes no distinction between God's justice, which redeems us at the cross, His holiness, which we share, or His righteousness, which we display.

Justice is the river that flows from the heart of God, responding to our sin and sinfulness in all its private and public manifestations. A theology that puts a wedge between personal holiness and prophetic advocacy uses the Bible to build a dam in that river.

Don't you have to be a specialist?

Simply put, justice isn't politics. It's far more than that. Justice is righteousness responding to wrong.

11

And this means that doing justice is central to the Christian faith. God's justice marks us out by the way we walk at work and play. Everyone can act justly.

People who act justly are known in the workplace to be the kind of people who deal fairly with friends and foe alike. Acting justly means that we do everything in our power to ensure that we all belong to a society in which righteousness exists in our social systems and businesses as much as in our public and private worlds.

God's justice is more than a message. It's God's mission to a broken world.

Working it out

Compare the two sections of Scripture below. What lessons can we draw from the relationship between justice and righteousness?

Psalm 72:1–4
1 Endow the king with your justice, O God,
the royal son with your righteousness.
2 He will judge your people in righteousness,
your afflicted ones with justice.
3 The mountains will bring prosperity to the people,
the hills the fruit of righteousness.
4 He will defend the afflicted among the people
and save the children of the needy;
he will crush the oppressor.

Romans 3:21–26
21But now a righteousness from God, apart from law, has been made known, to which the Law and the Prophets testify. 22This righteousness from God comes through faith in Jesus Christ to

all who believe. There is no difference, [23]for all have sinned and fall short of the glory of God, [24]and are justified freely by his grace through the redemption that came by Christ Jesus. [25]God presented him as a sacrifice of atonement, through faith in his blood. He did this to demonstrate his justice, because in his forbearance he had left the sins committed beforehand unpunished – [26]he did it to demonstrate his justice at the present time, so as to be just and the one who justifies those who have faith in Jesus.

Loving mercy

Is it possible that those who experience our ministry will have the slightest suspicion that God really cares for them?
Moss Nthla, General Secretary, South African
Evangelical Alliance

It's really hard to teach someone about mercy. Mercy is innate to our humanity, and when it goes the very meaning of being human is undermined.

Thank you, Mr Policeman!

I was the middle driver in a convoy of three cars driving in a great hurry at 2 am. Suddenly the bright light behind me, which I thought was coming from the third car in our convoy, went blue and started flashing. Before long an exasperated policeman drew up alongside me and indicated that I should pull over. When I did he told me to wind down my window and addressed me by name! He asked if I knew what speed I was driving at. I had spasmodic amnesia. Then he told me to drive home safely and not to be stupid. To my amazement he added, 'And you can tell your friend Mr Francis in the TR7 in front of you to watch himself.' Finally he waved me on.

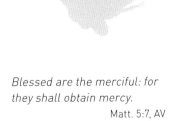

Blessed are the merciful: for they shall obtain mercy.
Matt. 5:7, AV

I couldn't believe it. He had me cold and yet there was no caution, no booking or even a command to report to my nearest police station. Just a tired policeman showing mercy. And for months to follow I loved all policemen!

Our biblical understanding of mercy begins at the mercy seat between the wings of the angels over the ark of the covenant (Exod. 25:17–22, AV), and is ultimately best demonstrated at the cross of Christ. No deed done on earth has ever demonstrated mercy so fully and unconditionally. But for us God's mercy is delivered in fresh supplies each day.

Pass it on

And the people who should best show mercy are those who have received it. The Christian walk should therefore be typified by delight in showing mercy. Those who do so are the first to restore rather than condemn. The first to forgive rather than keep scores. The first to befriend the workmate or immigrant.

People will know God is mercy only when they see mercy in us.

Working it out

Take some time to discuss two questions:

- When did someone last show you an act of mercy?

- What was your response to this?

Is it weak to be meek?

Most of us have a problem with humility. It smacks of weakness and subordination. Humility struggles in our culture of self-esteem and does little for our career development. In a celebrity culture it has been denounced as outdated.

What Churchill said about Attlee: 'He is a very humble man with a great deal to be humble about!'

What Attlee said about Churchill: 'There but for the grace of God goes God.'

Winston Churchill was Britain's war hero prime minister who was famous for his great speeches demonstrating his spirit of adventure. Clement Attlee was a less prominent political figure, and the two could be very critical of each other. They seemed to exemplify different approaches to humility.

Christians need to strike a balance between looking like weaklings and parading false modesty in an effort to look humble. But the fact is that you can't be meek if you're weak. Humility presupposes an element of influence or even power over other people. And it doesn't help to have a false sense of modesty either. That is only a façade that fades under pressure. The walk of humility is what makes justice and mercy flow naturally from us to others – even to people in faraway places we are never likely to meet.

Blessed are the meek, for they will inherit the earth.
Matt. 5:5

As we will see later in our studies, humility shouldn't be confused with self-deprecation. Rather, it's the ability and the willingness to put myself and my influence at someone else's disposal. And what makes this kind of humility so transformational is that it is humility exercised in God's presence for the benefit of others.

In the next three studies we will continue to explore these lifestyle themes. Our studies will weave together biblical reflections, worship, prayer, and insights on justice from a range of contributors. But we will also have an opportunity to explore what these themes mean for us through small group or church activities.

Our time together will explore, too, how you might be involved in and add your voice to Micah 2010 – our poverty reduction campaign. You will discover how you can get plugged in to the campaign – not just as a one-off event but as a future lifestyle. Let the Spirit lead you to make a difference.

A prayer for humility

May the mind of Christ my Saviour
Live in me from day to day,
By His love and power controlling
All I do and say.

May the peace of God my Father
Rule my life in everything,
That I may be calm to comfort
Sick and sorrowing.

May the love of Jesus fill me,
As the waters fill the sea;
Him exalting, self abasing,
This is victory.

May His beauty rest upon me
As I seek the lost to win,
And may they forget the channel,
Seeing only Him.

Kate Barclay Wilkinson

 FREE SONG DOWNLOAD
Visit www.micah2010.org to download Andy Bromley's song 'Love Mercy'.

Humility – walking softly before God

'And what does the LORD require of you? To ... walk humbly with your God.' (Micah 6:8)

'It's surprising how much you can accomplish if you don't care who gets the credit.' (Abraham Lincoln)

Micah's threefold challenge to us concludes with the idea of humility – but that's not because it's third in line. In fact it's the most fundamental of them because justice and mercy flow most naturally from those who have grasped the walk of humility. When humility goes missing the strong prey on the misfortunes of the weak. So let's continue our study with some biblical reflections on humility.

Daniel 4:19–31

[19] Then Daniel (also called Belteshazzar) was greatly perplexed for a time, and his thoughts terrified him. So the king said, 'Belteshazzar, do not let the dream or its meaning alarm you.' Belteshazzar answered, 'My lord, if only the dream applied to your enemies and its meaning to your adversaries! [20] The tree you saw, which grew large and strong, with its top touching the sky, visible to the whole earth, [21] with beautiful leaves and abundant fruit, providing food for all, giving shelter to the beasts of the field, and

having nesting places in its branches for the birds of the air –
[22] you, O king, are that tree! You have become great and strong; your greatness has grown until it reaches the sky, and your dominion extends to distant parts of the earth.

[23] 'You, O king, saw a messenger, a holy one, coming down from heaven and saying, 'Cut down the tree and destroy it, but leave the stump, bound with iron and bronze, in the grass of the field, while its roots remain in the ground. Let him be drenched with the dew of heaven; let him live like the wild animals, until seven times pass by for him.'

[24] 'This is the interpretation, O king, and this is the decree the Most High has issued against my lord the king: [25] You will be driven away from people and will live with the wild animals; you will eat grass like cattle and be drenched with the dew of heaven. Seven times will pass by for you until you acknowledge that the Most High is sovereign over the kingdoms of men and gives them to anyone he wishes. [26] The command to leave the stump of the tree with its roots means that your kingdom will be restored to you when you acknowledge that Heaven rules. [27] Therefore, O king, be pleased to accept my advice: Renounce your sins by doing what is right, and your wickedness by being kind to the oppressed. It may be that then your prosperity will continue.'

[28] All this happened to King Nebuchadnezzar. [29] Twelve months later, as the king was walking on the roof of the royal palace of Babylon, [30] he said, 'Is not this the great Babylon I have built as the royal residence, by my mighty power and for the glory of my majesty?'

[31] The words were still on his lips when a voice came from heaven, 'This is what is decreed for you, King Nebuchadnezzar: Your royal authority has been taken from you.'

A king's escape clause

It's worth reviewing the entire chapter of Daniel for the full context. The ancient world of Babylon knew nothing of democracy. The king was the law. He could do virtually anything to anyone at any time.

When Babylon became the world's superstate, and at the height of his power, King Nebuchadnezzar had a dream about a tree. It was large and luscious. Its leaves reached up to heaven and the fruit provided by the tree fed animals and people alike. But there was a celestial decision to cut it down, sparing only the root and a modest stump. Nebuchadnezzar's disturbing dream created two problems. In the first place he had no idea what it meant. But his greater problem arrived when he actually discovered the meaning: his need for humility.

The king called for the prophet Daniel – a senior minister in his administration who, rumour had it, was the chief of magicians with the spirit of divination (Dan. 4:4–33). Daniel understood the dream and was reluctant to explain what it meant. The tree, it turned out, was the king, who had grown to be one of the most powerful and revered men on the earth. But he was becoming arrogant and lacking in humility. So a decision had been taken in heaven: it was that the king would be stripped of his power and turned out to the open fields to behave like an animal for as long as it took for him to come to his senses.

Daniel, however, offered the king an escape clause: 'Renounce your sins by doing what is right, and your wickedness by being kind to the oppressed. It may be that then your prosperity will continue' (Dan. 4:27).

Twelve months later the king looked around and began to brag about his wealth, power and influence. And his dream came to pass.

What happened to Nebuchadnezzar is significant. Of even greater importance for us, though, is the connection Daniel makes in his antidote (Dan. 4:27). It is the recognition that there was a direct correlation between Nebuchadnezzar's lack of humility and his treatment of the poor. It was his arrogance and this lack of humility that made the king impervious to justice.

This had also been Pharaoh's problem in the Exodus event, when Egypt ruled the ancient world and made slaves of the Hebrew people. What stood between their oppression and their freedom was a ruthless king whose heart had become hardened (Exod. 8:15,32; 9:7,12).

The Bible leaves us with a challenging idea: the way in which we treat those over whom we have power is a sure measure of our humility quota.

Working it out

- Spend some time discussing Daniel's 'escape clause' for the king (Dan. 4:27).

- How might such a link between humility and justice apply today?

The anti-bully syndrome

All of this takes us back to a very basic biblical idea: it is that power ultimately belongs to God and that no human being has the right to extort from others or trample on another person. The playground bully is motivated by the same arrogance as a monarch or prime minister who exploits his people for personal gain. Such people suffer from a chronic lack of humility.

There is enough wealth in our world to avoid hunger. There is no reason why half a million women should die every year in childbirth or why not all children have access to full-time primary education. There is no reason why women should be devalued in the workplace and beaten up in their homes. Child soldiers, exploited children and human trafficking are all products of the same bullying syndrome which springs from a failure to walk humbly before God.

Powerful people in influential places act in their own interests. Through political intrigue, self-interest, party political preferences or tribalism, people in marble offices sit in leather chairs and make conscious decisions that destroy other people's lives. Their actions reveal a fundamental lack of humility that fails to recognise any greater accountability than their own self-interest.

Christians and secular humanists both want to see humanity flourish. Our faith in God leads us to understand that the best way to achieve this is by a walk of humility before God that is committed to other people's wellbeing.

The call to humility is God's call to everyone who exercises power. This is precisely why the early Christians were urged to pray for those in authority (Rom. 13:1–7; Titus 3:1; 1 Pet. 2:13–17). It's easy enough to suppose that these ideas about submission to authority came simply from a Church crippled by mindless obedience. But this is far from the truth. These injunctions were given to believers who were willing to lay down their lives because they followed Christ. There is no hint of compliance in the New Testament. There was, however, a powerful idea that even despots were allowed to rule by permission. When Christians showed obedience within the legal and moral law they were doing everything in their power to help the emperor carry out God's mandate for a society fit for human flourishing. Obedient citizenship undermined the need for political oppression.

When Christians couldn't vote, their prayers and acts of civil obedience were acts of citizenship. Sunday worship was bound up with political awareness.

No contest

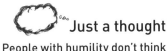

Just a thought

People with humility don't think less of themselves, they just think of themselves less.

Ken Blanchard and Norman Vincent Peale[1]

Of course, the most natural thing is to assume that humility is best achieved by comparing ourselves to God. Standing next to God is the easiest way to feel small. Comparisons with God's holiness are guaranteed to keep us in our place. And for too many of us this leaves us feeling morally inferior – without any corresponding response to the poor. We go no further than accepting we are fallible.

And it's just as easy to compare ourselves with someone in our family or our church who has a lot to brag about but never seems to do so. Most of us know somebody better than us who never makes a fuss about it. Often it's enough for them just to enter the room where we are for us to be reminded of the need for humility.

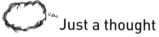

Just a thought

[God] is as high above a caterpillar as he is above an archangel.

A.W. Tozer

But, as Nebuchadnezzar discovered, biblical humility is far more radical and demanding than that. It does not insist on moral contests with God or our neighbour, but rather asks penetrating questions about how much we use our gifts and resources to serve the poor, 'the least of these' (Matt. 25:40) – or the person in the next pew.

Walking humbly before God means serving as better parents, managers or bus drivers. It makes us leaders who are more concerned about developing others than wondering what they give.

This is absolutely not a political message. It actually goes to the very heart of Christian worship and was captured for us in one of the best worship songs in the New Testament.

Philippians 2:4–11
4 Each of you should look not only to your own interests, but also to the interests of others.
5 Your attitude should be the same as that of Christ Jesus:
6 Who, being in very nature God,
did not consider equality with God something to be grasped,
7 but made himself nothing,
taking the very nature of a servant,
being made in human likeness.
8 And being found in appearance as a man,
he humbled himself
and became obedient to death –
even death on a cross!
9 Therefore God exalted him to the highest place
and gave him the name that is above every name,
10 that at the name of Jesus every knee should bow,
in heaven and on earth and under the earth,

[11] and every tongue confess that Jesus Christ is Lord,
to the glory of God the Father.

A reflection

'Kenosis means to empty oneself, throw off the rank of God, as if
a sovereign were to leave his throne and mantle and everything,
and dress in peasant rags to go among the peasants without
disrupting them with his presence as a king. Christ dressed himself
in humanity and appears as an ordinary man. If Christ were to
present himself here, in the cathedral, among the people that have
the goodness to be listening to me, I would not recognise him. And
knowing that he was the Son of God in the form of a man! And even
more than that it wasn't enough for him to look like a man, but he
also humiliated himself to take on the form of a slave to die like a
slave, crucified on a cross, like a thief, like a castoff of Israel who
was to be crucified outside the city like trash. This is Christ, the God
that humiliated himself through this kenosis, through this profound
emptying of who he was.'

Archbishop Oscar Romero, 1 October 1978

Working it out

In small groups explore the relationship between Micah's
message (Micah 6:6–8) and Paul's hymn of praise (Phil. 2:4—11).

A story of humility

Anyone who has visited a 'poor community' will know how the
dynamics of power works between the 'haves' and 'have nots'.
Radical biblical humility is likely to call for a reordering of our
relationships. In his excellent book *Walking with the Poor*[2] Bryant
Myers tells of an encounter which showed the power of humility.

When Ravi Jayakaran, the Indian development specialist, visited a village in India, the villagers did the customary thing and put out two seats – one for him and one for a colleague. The villagers sat on the floor mats. To their amazement Ravi and his colleague put the chairs aside and joined them on the dusty mats. The two listened closely to the villagers as they talked about the variety of projects in the village.

At the end of the conversation Ravi asked the villagers what they felt to be the key lessons learned from the meeting. 'You are sitting on the same mat, looking me in the eye and talking to us as equals,' said an elderly man. This encounter with two apparently powerful professionals who chose to sit on a dirty mat turned out to be more transformational than them turning up to dig a well or build a school. The key change was the relationship, which empowered the villagers to think of themselves as equals. This is biblical humility.

Worshipping with humility

Our time together with Micah aims to draw us into words, worship and works that reflect God's heartbeat for the poor. And the humility that Micah was so passionate about goes right to the very heart of our worship today. Increasingly Christian artists and worship leaders have found themselves on that journey, and our study gives us an opportunity to join them. Paul Baloche says:

'This whole idea about walking humbly with God ... it's got me thinking. It's almost as if you want to turn that scripture backwards – to make it read that, as we walk humbly with the Lord, it's as if our heart is brought into line. In turn that gives us compassion and mercy towards others when we see them messing up. Instead of jumping on

The kind of humility which cries to God because of my sin and ignores the sin of oppression fails the Nebuchadnezzar test.

them, we're in a state of submission to the Lord, a state where we're aware of our shortcomings and failures. And it drives us towards fighting for justice for others, since the greater the awareness we have of what God has done for us, the more hungry we are that others are able to live their lives free from oppression and injustice and better able to soak up more of the good things that God intends for all.'[3]

Worship filled with biblical humility cannot speak to God and be deaf to the world. The kind of humility which cries to God because of my sin and ignores the sin of oppression fails the Nebuchadnezzar test. It does not acknowledge that we also have a responsibility to pray for and respond to the arrogant power that oppresses the poor. The same passion which drives me to personal humility is the passion that should rise up against our institutions and systems that lack the humility to care for the oppressed.

When we walk with the oppressed in our worship we are walking humbly with God and we are responding to Micah's challenge.

Just a thought

The beauty of our prayers, songs and music or the dignity of or solemnity of religious services do not in themselves please God. God is looking for a deeper kind of music, a richer kind of liturgy: the music of our obedience, and the daily liturgy of loving our neighbour. Lips and life need to agree.

Graham Kendrick[4]

Working it out

Perhaps the most powerful symbol Jesus ever gave us for humility in the midst of a worship setting was the towel and the bowl in which He washed His disciples' feet (John 13:4–5).

Imagine that you are in a creative Christian company of three partners. Look again at Paul Baloche's statement (opposite).

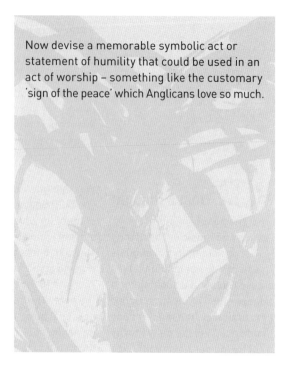

Now devise a memorable symbolic act or statement of humility that could be used in an act of worship – something like the customary 'sign of the peace' which Anglicans love so much.

A global prayer on 10.10.10

There is no greater expression of humility than the act of prayer. Prayer for ourselves is important but it's even more important to approach God on behalf of others. October 2010 sees 100 million Christians across over forty nations repeating a simple prayer which puts God's agenda for justice at the centre of our worship events. Imagine what God will be able to do through us for the poor as our expressions of humility and prayer become an integral part of our worship.

The prayer is based on Nehemiah's prayer of confession (Neh. 1:5–11), which he prayed at the very outset of his own ministry. As you pray this prayer it's worth remembering that it is meant to see change take place for many millions in the years ahead. Our passion and prayers for justice may be an anthem to misery or a note of confident hope in a God who really cares about our world and the people in it.

But remember, too, that our prayers are meant to include our actions – as much as our sincerity.

The 24-7 Prayer movement is right behind Micah 2010. I wholeheartedly urge you to join this global chorus of prayer for the poorest people on earth. Together we can make a little history.

Pete Greig, 24-7 Prayer/Alpha International

Micah 2010 prayer

O Lord, our great and awesome God, loyal to Your promise of love and faithful to all who honour and obey You,
hear our prayer.
We pray for those who live in poverty,
we cry out for those who are denied justice, and we weep for all who are suffering.
We confess that we have not always obeyed You.
We have neglected Your commands and have ignored Your call for justice.
We have been guided by self-interest and lived in spiritual poverty.
Forgive us.
We remember Your promises to fill the hungry with good things,
to redeem the land by Your mighty hand, and to restore peace.
Father God, help us always to proclaim Your justice and mercy with humility so that, by the power of Your Spirit, we can rid the world of the sin of extreme poverty.
As part of Your global Church, we stand with millions who praise and worship You.
May our words and deeds declare Your perfect goodness, love and righteousness to both the powerful and the powerless so that Your kingdom may come on earth as it is in heaven.
Amen.

Working it out

Give some time in your small groups to reflect on this prayer.

- How might it serve your local church – not just on 10.10.10 but as a source of corporate transformation? The prayer is meant as a tool for worship which prompts and promotes our walk of humility.

- Make sure you take a look at www.micah2010.org for the resources to enrich our worship. Why not go straight to the website and explore the material together during the meeting?

One thing! A personal commitment

Much of our time has been focused on big themes. We have even plugged into the big idea of 100 million people praying. So it's quite easy to get lost in the crowds. But this is an opportunity for personal reflection in which to ask, 'What does the Lord require of *me*?'

The idea here is not to spend time feeling guilty about what we haven't done. It is to open our hearts and to ask what it is that God is asking each of us to do.

Working it out

So here is your personal task. As you reflect on the kind of humility which serves others, ask: 'What is the *one* thing I should do in order to make a difference to someone else's life?'

And remember, God isn't a compulsive bully. It really doesn't have to hurt to be transformational. He never makes a hard ask without giving us the grace to respond.

Let me give you a personal example. When we were asked to pray and consider what was the *one* thing we would do as a result of a three-day leadership meeting my response was to join Facebook! Yes, I know! You're wondering if God really is that bothered about me telling the world where I went on holiday. But it was a lot more to do with my attitude than anything else. The outcome is that it's been fun. And now my kids know what I'm up to, I have rediscovered a work colleague I hadn't spoken to for thirty years, and I get to encourage and support a whole family of friends around the world.

At the back of this book there is a list of resources you can draw from as you give some thought to what it is that the Lord requires from you.

Thinking about next week

Our time together will focus on mercy. As a key part of the exercise we plan to focus on the story of the unmerciful servant in Matthew 18:21–35. Three people will be required to help us with this exercise and prepare a brief drama. They will need to look at the passage and prepare their particular roles. And don't forget it's a story showing kingdom principles about mercy and forgiveness.

One person will assume the role of the unmerciful servant.

A second will be the fellow servant he had imprisoned for owing him a small sum. You will want to know why the unmerciful servant was unable to extend forgiveness.

The third is the interrogation officer. In this interrogation He will want to ask what the prisoner – the unmerciful servant – felt about his behaviour. He will need to find out whether he really could have paid the king and why it took so long to pay his debt – particularly as he had enough to lend to someone else.

 FREE SONG DOWNLOAD
Visit www.micah2010.org to download Tim Hughes' song 'We Must Go'.

Notes

[1] Ken Blanchard and Norman Vincent Peale, *The Power of Ethical Management* (New York: William Morrow, 1988).

[2] Bryant L. Myers, *Walking with the Poor* (London: Orbis Books, 1999).

[3] Paul Baloche in *The Art of Compassion*, Compassion Art (Hodder & Stoughton (UK), Faith Words (US), 2009). Used by permission.

[4] Graham Kendrick, *The Art of Compassion*, ibid.

Mercy – getting a second chance

'And what does the LORD require of you? To ... love mercy ...' (Micah 6:8)

Today, it falls to a new generation to work for justice and a fairer world. Globally, we need education, awareness and action on poverty. Governments must work together, give more, and make aid more effective. The corporate world must contribute its creativity and energies to the challenges of development and eradicating poverty. And communities across the world need to mobilise to bring people and resources together, to bring about change.

The work of Micah Challenge, and the wider Make Poverty History movement, is essential to building a better future and a more just world.

Kevin Rudd, Prime Minister of Australia

ercy is inescapable for anyone who has met with God. His mercy and His compassion owe nothing to anyone or anything beyond Himself. But there is no such thing as mercy without a recognition that without it our lives would be destitute wastelands.

And the amazing thing is that He has drawn us in to share this quality of mercy with everyone we meet. Mercy was graphically shown to us in the ark of the covenant.

Exodus 25:17–22

[17] Make an atonement cover of pure gold – two and a half cubits long and a cubit and a half wide. [18] And make two cherubim out of hammered gold at the ends of the cover. [19] Make one cherub on one end and the second cherub on the other; make the cherubim of one piece with the cover, at the two ends. [20] The cherubim are to have their wings spread upwards, overshadowing the cover with them. The cherubim are to face each other, looking towards the cover. [21] Place the cover on top of the ark and put in the ark the Testimony, which I will give you. [22] There, above the cover between the two cherubim that are over the ark of the Testimony, I will meet with you and give you all my commands for the Israelites.

Working it out

In your group consider the inherent tension in this passage.

• Why there is a need for atonement and what is atonement (see Lev. 16; 17:11; 1 Pet. 3:18)?

• How does this contrast with the idea in verse 22 of God meeting with Moses and the high priests?

• The covering is also known as the 'mercy seat'. Discuss the reason for this.

The mercy seat [AV] was foundational in teaching that God had a merciful relationship with His covenant people – a belief that is repeated throughout the Psalms and the prophetic books of the Bible. Again and again it is clear from the tone and context of the Scriptures that mercy can't be taught. It flows from our proximity to the heart of God and it flourishes in the lives of those who understand what it means to be forgiven. Jeremiah's writing expresses this really well.

Lamentations 3:22–24

²² Because of the LORD's great love we are not consumed,
    for his compassions never fail.
²³ They are new every morning;
    great is your faithfulness.
²⁴ I say to myself, 'The LORD is my portion;
    therefore I will wait for him.

Here is a prayer from King David that we can pray together.

Psalm 51

¹ Have mercy on me, O God,
    according to your unfailing love;
  according to your great compassion
    blot out my transgressions.
² Wash away all my iniquity
    and cleanse me from my sin.
³ For I know my transgressions,
    and my sin is always before me.
⁴ Against you, you only, have I sinned
    and done what is evil in your sight,
    so that you are proved right when you speak
    and justified when you judge.
⁵ Surely I was sinful at birth,
    sinful from the time my mother conceived me.
⁶ Surely you desire truth in the inner parts;
    you teach me wisdom in the inmost place.
⁷ Cleanse me with hyssop, and I shall be clean;
    wash me, and I will be whiter than snow.
⁸ Let me hear joy and gladness;
    let the bones you have crushed rejoice.
⁹ Hide your face from my sins
    and blot out all my iniquity.
¹⁰ Create in me a pure heart, O God,
    and renew a steadfast spirit within me.
¹¹ Do not cast me from your presence
    or take your Holy Spirit from me.
¹² Restore to me the joy of your salvation
    and grant me a willing spirit, to sustain me.
¹³ Then I will teach transgressors your ways,
    and sinners will turn back to you.

We need to recapture the gospel glow of the early Christians, who were non-conformists in the truest sense of the word and refused to shape their witness according to the mundane patterns of the world. Willingly they sacrificed fame, fortune, and life itself in behalf of a cause they knew to be right. Quantitatively small, they were qualitatively giants. Their powerful gospel put an end to such barbaric evils as infanticide and bloody gladiatorial contests. Finally, they captured the Roman Empire for Jesus Christ.

Martin Luther King Jnr,
Strength to Love[1]

14 Save me from bloodguilt, O God,
　　the God who saves me,
　　and my tongue will sing of your
　　　　righteousness.
15 O Lord, open my lips,
　　and my mouth will declare your praise.
16 You do not delight in sacrifice, or I would
　　　　bring it;
　　you do not take pleasure in burnt offerings.
17 The sacrifices of God are a broken spirit;
　　a broken and contrite heart,
　　O God, you will not despise.
18 In your good pleasure make Zion prosper;
　　build up the walls of Jerusalem.
19 Then there will be righteous sacrifices,
　　whole burnt offerings to delight you;
　　then bulls will be offered on your altar.

This concept of mercy is very central to who Jesus is and what He did. One of the best-known stories in the New Testament screams uncompromising mercy and still stands as a powerful lesson for all of us.

Matthew 18:23–35
23 Therefore, the kingdom of heaven is like a king who wanted to settle accounts with his servants. 24 As he began the settlement, a man who owed him ten thousand talents was brought to him. 25 Since he was not able to pay, the master ordered that he and his wife and his children and all that he had be sold to repay the debt.
26 The servant fell on his knees before him. 'Be patient with me,' he begged, 'and I will pay back everything.' 27 The servant's master took pity on him, cancelled the debt and let him go.
28 But when that servant went out, he found one of his fellow-servants who owed him a hundred denarii. He grabbed him and began to choke him. 'Pay back what you owe me!' he demanded.
29 His fellow-servant fell to his knees and

begged him, 'Be patient with me, and I will pay you back.'
[30] But he refused. Instead, he went off and had the man thrown into prison until he could pay the debt. [31] When the other servants saw what had happened, they were greatly distressed and went and told their master everything that had happened.
[32] Then the master called the servant in. 'You wicked servant,' he said, 'I cancelled all that debt of yours because you begged me to. [33] Shouldn't you have had mercy on your fellow-servant just as I had on you?' [34] In anger his master turned him over to the jailers to be tortured, until he should pay back all he owed.
[35] This is how my heavenly Father will treat each of you unless you forgive your brother from your heart.

Mercy and forgiveness

The disciples triggered this story with a question about forgiveness (Matt. 18:21). The rabbis taught that a person was to forgive three times. Peter, no doubt believing he was showing generosity, suggested seven times. Jesus' response was, as always, well beyond human expectations. He recommended seventy times seven. The point is that it would take a particularly callous person to keep that kind of score sheet. It was Jesus' way of saying, 'Forget the score card. Do it all the time!'

And then He told them the story about mercy and forgiveness. It's really important to remember that this isn't so much a moral story about how nice it is to forgive but a far more radical reminder of the kingdom principles that Jesus was so keen to profile.

The king's bank and the businessman

A king with huge resources was in the process of settling his accounts and was evidently keen to start with those with the highest debt. So he called in the fellow who owed him a small fortune. Which means that this debtor was no peasant. In Jesus' mind this was a wealthy businessman who was himself in a position to grant small loans to others. He could have been anything from a merchant banker to a tax collector or trader. Possibly he started owing a modest debt that increased over a long period of time with interest charges. What is clear is that he had become a very privileged person and, for whatever reason, he had neglected to pay his debt on time. The king therefore did what he was legally entitled to do: he threatened him with slavery.

And this led to the biggest begging exhibition the town square had seen in weeks. It's not difficult to imagine the poor people who were listening to Jesus enjoying the idea of a wealthy man begging for his life. Which is precisely when Jesus would have turned the tables on His audience. For while they were still giggling at the idea, Jesus highlighted the power of mercy and forgiveness. Not only did the king listen to this man but he did something even more extraordinary: he cancelled the debt entirely! More than the man had asked for. The crowds were probably disappointed.

And this is mercy at work. It doesn't always please everyone. For in an exacting and often vindictive world people generally want to know that other people will be punished – especially if they are privileged people who have done wrong. This is why the world has become hostile to investment bankers who receive huge bonuses in the midst of an economic downturn that their greed created. Even if the man owing the money wasn't particularly rich, why should such an accumulated debt be wiped out rather than deferred? Mercy really is outrageous.

Repaying loving kindness

We're not meant to like this man very much. There is something so self-possessed about him that he is unable to transfer the same kindness he had received. And again, this is what makes mercy so extraordinary: God shows mercy to unlikeable types of people. So when this businessman met a fellow servant who owed him a small debt he had the man thrown into prison. The king was outraged when the news reached him. In fact so outraged that he had him imprisoned and interrogated until the debt was repaid – which probably meant he could have paid it in the first place.

The king remained the same king – just and merciful, but also outraged. And his rage had nothing to do with needing his money back. It was because this man had failed to show mercy in the same way that he had received it (Matt. 18:33). It's also really important to note that this is not a story about personal sins or moral failure. Jesus has deliberately given us an example to do with commercial enterprise. Too often our preaching shies away from relating righteousness to our financial or commercial institutions, but Jesus is not reluctant to do so. The Bible has more to say about money than it does about issues of human sexuality, marriage or personal morality.

The principle of the kingdom is this: those who have received mercy must show it in return. Mercy which stops at the mercy seat where we worship fails to impress the King.

It's important to say that people who never claim to know or even care about God can also be those who demonstrate mercy. Even with our fallen nature it is clearly a part of what it means to have been made in the image of God. But mercy which is initiated by God will always respond by drawing attention to God and not to ourselves.

Working it out

Last week a number of people were asked to prepare a brief drama to help us explore the story we have just been focusing on from the perspective of the unforgiving servant. The aim is to try to get inside his head to see what we can learn about our own response to showing mercy. We will follow him to the interrogation session of the prison.

One person will assume the role of the unmerciful servant.

A second will be the fellow servant he had imprisoned for owing a small sum. You will want to know why the unmerciful servant was unable to extend forgiveness.

The third is the interrogation officer. He will want to ask what the prisoner – the unmerciful servant – felt about his behaviour. He will need to find out whether he really could have paid the king and why it took so long to pay his debt – particularly as he had enough to lend to someone else.

A story of mercy – Jubilee 2000

One the most powerful movements to have come to public prominence in the mid 1990s was Jubilee 2000. Drop the Debt was a call to powerful bodies such as the World Bank and the International Monetary Fund to drop the unpayable debts of forty-three highly indebted poor countries (HIPC). These poor nations owed such unbearable debts to rich nations and institutions such as the World Bank that they were not able to provide resources for education or health and were unlikely to repay the debts for generations to come.

In response a Debt Crisis Network reshaped itself into a broad coalition to become the Jubilee 2000 campaign. Jubilee 2000 had at its heart a biblical message of freedom (Lev. 25). It was influenced by Christian organisations such as CAFOD, Christian Aid and Tearfund. At the 1998 meeting of G8 nations in Birmingham, Jubilee 2000 mounted one of the most significant public responses to debt relief as 70,000 people formed a human chain. Over a three-year period Christian response to indebtedness helped to reposition the Christian message as a message of mercy and provided an impetus for Make Poverty History and other campaigning ministries, such as Micah Challenge.

At its final meeting in December 2000 the British Chancellor was clear that Christian involvement had made a substantial difference to public attitudes to the poor.

Showing mercy in small settings, as much as the big stories of acts of mercy, will help people understand the God of mercy we have come to know.

Working it out

One of the exciting features of the Christian faith today is the fact that God has raised up so many mercy ministries.

- Spend some time in groups identifying as many of them as possible in your nation or community.

- Now spend some time praying for them. Ministries of this kind are always overwhelmed by the size of the task and never have enough resources to meet the huge needs.

As you pray, keep an open mind to whatever God may be saying to you about your involvement with them beyond this session.

Just a thought

I have always found that mercy bears richer fruits than strict justice.

Abraham Lincoln

COMPASSIONART
CREATING FREEDOM FROM POVERTY

I can't bear it. I'm missing her. I have her photo on my piano. Another's in the studio. I can't get her out of my mind. I've got my own children to think about and look out for. What's going on? Is this what a breakdown looks like? Is that what I'm having here?

Martin Smith[2]

Worship with mercy

In Exodus 25 the link between mercy and worship could not be clearer for us. How could we possibly miss it so frequently? And yet we do. But God is working with us to take us back to true worship. We who have obtained mercy are being called to show mercy in return.

Let's reflect on three brief statements from the CompassionArt team.

Martin Smith was foundational in getting the project together. His journey, which drove him

If we use our whole selves to give God what he deserves – not just with hands raised and a song sung with passion, but with hands outstretched ready to work and bring answers – how much more could we achieve?

Darlene Zschech[3]

Like the words that Micah gives in chapter 6 verse 8, we need to get active with our mercy – to love it, but not passively from the sidelines. The way we show that we love mercy should result in lives being transformed and nothing less.

Tim Hughes[4]

more deeply into mercy, is a powerful record of walking with the Spirit. This journey began when he met a young girl in India called Farin. Little wonder he called his daughter Mary-Anna Merciful.

Darlene Zschech is a writer who has written some of our most influential songs and who has developed a passion to embrace social justice as an integral part of her worship and ministry.

Tim Hughes made a very important journey from worshipping without taking his own words seriously to weighing what God was saying about the poor and putting this in the very centre of the room. His journey has been to make mercy and justice a main event in every act of worship.

Working it out

- What do you make of these statements?

- Are these things much easier for Christian celebrities to say, or do the statements hold any genuine lessons for us?

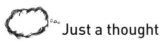 **Just a thought**
Music can change the world because it can change people.
Bono

A global promise on 10.10.10

Last week we introduced our global prayer. But after we have prayed then what? As we have just discussed, our worship is incomplete without our actions. We trust you will want to take that further step with us on 10.10.10 when we are hoping to have ten million people making practical promises to God concerning the poor.

The idea is still to have this as an integral part of our act of worship. We can imagine the impact of mercy if ten million Christians promise to do something small but meaningful as a part of our act of worship.

The promise should follow the prayer. It would be good for the group to go through this prayer together. Ask someone to play the leader's role.

Promise box

The leader says:
As Christians we want to remember the poor, act with justice and speak up for the voiceless. We support the promise made ten years ago by world leaders to bring half a billion people out of extreme poverty by 2015.
With five years to go we will not forget this commitment to children, women and men whose God-given potential is smothered by poverty. We believe there is a reason for hope. We promise to remind our leaders of what they have committed to do.
Today let us join 100 million Christians around the world in prayer and promise to see poverty halved by 2015.

Everyone joins in the promise:
We promise to remember the poor.
We promise to remind our leaders to keep their commitment to the poor.
As a sign of our promise we make this handprint.
Together, our hands are a message to our leaders to act with justice and remember the poor.

Because worship is about actions of mercy we have a whole list of practical steps we want to follow through together.

10.10.10 is an opportunity to demonstrate that wherever we may be in the world we are all standing together as Christians, recommitting ourselves to the pursuit of justice and encouraging action from our leaders. It's a global moment, which we hope means that a church in rural France, a mega-church in Nairobi and a suburban church in Lima are all crying out with one voice.

2010 marks ten years since nations of the world promised to meet the Millennium Development Goals – we have only five years to go to make the eight goals a reality. The task is urgent and we encourage all Christians to take part in the promise as a solemn personal covenant so that the impact is lasting – not just for one day.

The promise is simple to organise: the words are given in the box above and as a sign of the promise we are asking people to raise their hands in promise, then make a special handprint.

Hands signify worship, hands pledge support, and we use our hands to demonstrate God's love. The action of using our handprint to confirm our promise is a symbol of faith and action coming together. It can be done by children and adults of all ages, and by people who cannot read or write.

The five fingers on our hand represent five years to go till 2015 and remind us that the task is urgent. The handprints are also a visible message to pass on to our leaders so that our promise to halve global poverty cannot be forgotten.

We believe the promise will work well in your local church or group, and also provides the opportunity for you to link with and reach out to others to encourage them to get involved.

We encourage everyone who makes a promise and handprint to get involved in the big handover so that our actions can have an impact on our leaders. We do not want them to forget the promise to halve global poverty by 2015. See 'The big handover' on page 54.

Working it out

Take some time to consider how you and your church might put these creative ideas in place.

If you think your group or church has come up with an all-time great idea worth sharing, do write in to us. Put your ideas on the website www.micah2010.org

What part can I play?

Once again this is your opportunity to ask what God is saying to you about mercy. Is there 'one thing' you need to do or change to make a difference? It is also perfectly possible that there is nothing new for you to consider.

A prayer for mercy

Merciful Father,
we cry out to You for those whose lives are destroyed by poverty,
malnutrition and disease.
We pray for those living in areas where drought and famine are a
way of life;
for children whose mothers do not understand basic nutrition
and for those too young or too ill to pray for themselves. Have mercy
on them, O Lord, we pray. Amen.

 FREE SONG DOWNLOAD
Visit www.micah2010.org to download Brenton Brown's song
'Jesus You Are Worthy'.

Notes

[1] Martin Luther King Jnr, *Strength to Love* (London: Hodder and Stoughton, 1964).

[2] Martin Smith, in *The Art of Compassion*, Compassion Art (Hodder & Stoughton (UK), Faith Words (US), 2009). Used by permission.

[3] Darlene Zschech, in *The Art of Compassion*, ibid.

[4] Tim Hughes, in *The Art of Compassion*, ibid.

Justice – righteousness responding to wrong

'And what does the Lord require of you? To act justly ...' (Micah 6:8)

The Millennium Development Goals are far too immense for just one or even a few individuals to take on alone. We must work together to create the clarity of vision to effectively obtain our objectives on the pressing issues that face us today. Positive, prayerful advocacy provides the momentum necessary to get important issues on the table and make the changes we so desperately require ... I commend you on your service, support and contribution to the needs of others, according to the grace of God.

John McKay, Canadian politician

Group work?

Our study has walked backward to Micah's starting point: to act justly. How does that word 'justly' make you feel? It is actually a deliberately 'feely' question. And that's because most of us respond emotionally rather than biblically to the question of justice.

As we said in our opening study, there are some very good reasons for this. The notion of justice sounds like a radical political agenda which never gets discussed in polite company. A sermon on justice would have the same effect as the preacher saying, 'We're looking for snakes!' Three people would love the idea. Everybody else would be running for the door. We are much more comfortable talking about 'holiness' or 'righteousness', which appear to have far fewer political overtones.

But there is a clear relationship in the Bible between 'righteousness', 'justice' and holiness. In fact it would be a great exercise to go through your Bible or a concordance and see just how often 'justice' and 'righteousness' sit side by side.

Psalm 72:1–4
> [1] Endow the king with your justice, O God,
>   the royal son with your righteousness.
> [2] He will judge your people in righteousness,
>   your afflicted ones with justice.
> [3] The mountains will bring prosperity to the people,
>   the hills the fruit of righteousness.
> [4] He will defend the afflicted among the people
>   and save the children of the needy;
>   he will crush the oppressor.

Working it out

Take some time to examine this passage from Psalm 72 together.

• How would you explain the relationship between justice and righteousness which appears in this passage?

• What range of responsibilities does this passage attach to the king?

- Is there any relationship between this passage and the events that surrounded Nebuchadnezzar in Daniel 4?

This idea of justice – righteousness responding to wrong – was central to Jesus' ministry as well as to the Early Church. Let's study another well-known Bible passage, which we may not immediately think of as a justice text. In fact we normally think about it for very different reasons.

Acts 6:1–7

[1]In those days when the number of disciples was increasing, the Grecian Jews among them complained against the Hebraic Jews because their widows were being overlooked in the daily distribution of food. [2]So the Twelve gathered all the disciples together and said, 'It would not be right for us to neglect the ministry of the word of God in order to wait on tables. [3]Brothers, choose seven men from among you who are known to be full of the Spirit and wisdom. We will turn this responsibility over to them [4]and will give our attention to prayer and the ministry of the word.' [5]This proposal pleased the whole group. They chose Stephen, a man full of faith and of the Holy Spirit; also Philip, Procorus, Nicanor, Timon, Parmenas, and Nicolas from Antioch, a convert to Judaism. [6]They presented these men to the apostles, who prayed and laid their hands on them.
[7]So the word of God spread. The number of disciples in Jerusalem increased rapidly, and a large number of priests became obedient to the faith.

Justice and the birth of the Church

This passage of the Bible may record the beginning of the diaconate – the appointment of those who serve as deacon-leaders in the congregation. But as far as Luke, the writer of Acts, was concerned, that's not really the point. In fact it's worth noting that the first serious tension in the Church arose not over an issue of theology but over one of injustice.

It was no accident that the Church had identified widows as a special target group to serve on a daily basis. In a culture where women were powerless without their husbands, widows and orphans were the lowest caste in society – and therefore the most vulnerable. This is why ministry to this group came to symbolise true religion (Prov. 31:8–9; James 1:27). And, in a predominantly Hebrew congregation, a Greek widow was in even more danger of being marginalised.

The purpose of this development was not to create a new structure of leadership; it was to register the fact that equal treatment of Greek and Jewish Christian widows was vitally important. So the Church stopped everything it was doing and organised a democratic meeting which appointed seven high-quality men, not necessarily to serve tables, but to supervise the work. At least three of them were high flyers with roving ministries. And before they knew it, Stephen had become the first Christian martyr.

If we are to be true to this section of Scripture, our structures, synods, protocols and titles make no sense to God or the watching world unless they aim to serve.

Although reconciliation with other people is not reconciliation with God, nor is social action evangelism, nor is political liberation salvation, nevertheless we affirm that evangelism and socio-political involvement are both part of our Christian duty.
Lausanne Covenant, 1974

It's a serious misreading of the story to say that the apostles were too busy to serve and therefore gave this lesser work away to others. The very opposite is true. This work was so important that the apostles knew that they themselves would have to do it unless they found other people of equal quality to take responsibility for this task.

That day, when the apostles laid their hands on these seven men, poverty alleviation was raised to the status of serious missions.

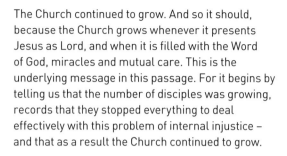

As a global Christian community seeking to live in obedience to Scripture, we recognise the challenge of poverty across God's world. We welcome the international initiative to halve world poverty by 2015, and pledge ourselves to do all we can, through our organisations and churches, to back this with prayerful, practical action in our nations and communities.

World Evangelical Alliance, 2001

The Church continued to grow. And so it should, because the Church grows whenever it presents Jesus as Lord, and when it is filled with the Word of God, miracles and mutual care. This is the underlying message in this passage. For it begins by telling us that the number of disciples was growing, records that they stopped everything to deal effectively with this problem of internal injustice – and that as a result the Church continued to grow.

But there was something else: even priests became obedient to the faith. This is quite an important statement for the priests were likely to be the most informed and therefore the most sceptical people in the community.

The problem with justice is that we have forgotten just how important it has been throughout Christian history. The very notion of justice was woven into our theology of the cross and the atonement. It led Christians to care for the poor, to set up hospitals and places of education and, despite resistance from within the Church, to abolish the slave trade. In many Western societies it was the Christian concern for justice that established the principles enshrined in our justice systems.

The contribution of the church to its members and community has brought about a renewal of the minds of people with a stronger commitment to the needs of their fellow men. All these auger well for the community in which we live and reflect positively on the quality of leadership in the church.

Dato' Seri Abdullah Haji Ahmad Badawi,
Prime Minister of Malaysia, Calvary Church, 2008

If we ignore the world we betray the word of God which sends us out to serve the world. If we ignore the word of God we have nothing to bring to the world. Justice and justification by faith, worship and political action, the spiritual and the material, personal change and structural change belong together. As in the life of Jesus, being, doing and saying are at the heart of our integral task.
Micah Network Conference, 2001

Getting in step with God

Thankfully there are real signals that Christians are moving towards showing God's heart for the poor and for justice, not as a supplement to their worship but as a central part of it.

In the past thirty years many key statements have been made by the Christian Church through which we have come to see again that justice is godly and that biblical Christian faith cannot treat it as an optional extra. This is the work of Integral Mission, which enables the local churches – particularly in poor nations – to blend the proclamation of the gospel with care of the poor and biblical activism. The kind of work represented by global Christian networks such as Micah Network (www.micahnetwork.org) and Integral Mission (www.integralmission.net) equips the Church in its work for justice.

But it's not just a matter of what we are saying; what really counts is what we are doing to make a difference and bring God's justice for the needy. When sceptics and political leaders see us in action it tells them of our commitment to people, but equally it tells them of our commitment to the God we serve.

Just A Thought

As well as our responsibility before God we also have a responsibility to our Governments. The challenge is to ask how we earth this not just in our organisation but also in our churches.
C.B. Samuels,
chair Micah Challenge India

Speaking up for the poor

Christian witness is growing increasingly to encompass not only practical action but also prophetic advocacy for the poor. Advocacy – speaking up for the poor – takes us a step beyond practical action to prophetic engagement. Quite frankly, it's not something we are always comfortable in doing. It looks on the face of it to be nothing more than political activism. However, there is a world of difference between political activism for ideological reasons and speaking to the powerful with and on behalf of the poor in the name of Christ. When Moses stood before Pharaoh and said 'Let my people go!' (Exod. 5:1) this was advocacy. Advocacy is the prophetic responsibility of standing against abuse, not for our own benefit but for the health of those who suffer. It does not come from political conviction but is the overflow behaviour of people who walk in biblical humility and who love mercy. It is reflected in the work of global movements such as International Justice Mission (www.ijm.org), which enter into situations of violence in order to provide legal support for vulnerable people who have been abused or tortured in secret.

> *We should not be surprised therefore that God specifically uses the work of justice as the pathway for liberating us from the Christian cul-de-sac of triviality and small fears.*
>
> Gary Haugen, International Justice Mission

But it is precisely this willingness to step out on the edge that attracts God's power in the gospel and draws the attention of those who wonder what good news really means to people who have no hope. Our advocacy is neither the easy nor the political option, but it is what righteousness demands.

Christian advocacy is the prophetic edge of the gospel and it takes our Christian community from the parochialism of our internal agendas to serving as pastors and carers of the human race.

Small acts of justice

Few of us will be called to do global acts of justice. Every day, however, these opportunities come to us in our neighbourhood, our families or our places of work. As we saw from the book of Acts, they certainly come to us within the context of the local church. So if you are an employer or in business, remember there is a call to act justly (Psa. 62:10). And equally, justice applies to us in dealing with neighbours and immigrants (Deut. 24:17) as much as orphans and widows (Deut. 10:18). In other words, justice is a low-hanging fruit that everyone can reach. Acting justly is not the task only of Christian specialists.

A just friend will be fair in dealing with arguments amongst other friends. A just boss will act impartially.

Working it out

How might we, as 'ordinary prophets', approach justice?

A story of 'ordinary prophets'

My first visit to Peru with the Christian charity Christian Aid filled me with vivid memories. One such memory is of a visit to the Andean region of Ayacucho. It was impressive to have my host point to a solitary building in the middle of a field and be told, 'That is a church.' The thought occurred to me that the Church really does have the ability to be where no one else is to be found!

I was even more moved when our car stopped on a main route leading to a nearby town. This time the driver pointed to a spot where three Christian missionaries had been killed by the revolutionary group known as the Shining Path. I was told that they gave their lives because they believed in justice for the marginalised people they came to serve.

Yet what struck me most of all during that visit were the remarkable stories of pastors being voted into power as local councillors and mayors. Was the Church becoming more politically involved, I asked. That wasn't exactly what was happening. It was that church leaders had become true citizens, taking on responsibility, not just for their own congregations, but for the wellbeing of those around. And because they were seen as honest and trustworthy people in their own communities, they were being voted into offices for which they were unprepared – and without even a theology to help them cope with their new positions.

The role of my host agency, Paz Y Esperanza (Peace and Hope), was to support these emerging 'ordinary prophets' in developing the skills they needed to take on the responsibilities which had been thrust upon them.

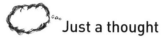

Just a thought

Faith without a commitment to justice for the poor is a sham because it ignores the most explicit of all the social concerns of Scripture.

Tony Campolo

A prayer for justice

We beg You, Lord,
to help and defend us.
Deliver the oppressed,
pity the insignificant,
raise the fallen,
show Yourself to the needy,
heal the sick,
bring back those of Your people
who have gone astray,
feed the hungry,
lift up the weak,
take off the prisoners' chains.
May every nation come to know
that You alone are God,
that Jesus Christ is Your Child,
that we are Your people,
the sheep that You pasture.

Clement of Rome

Worship with justice

What drove twelve well-known international Christian artists to suspend their programmes in order to write and record songs for which neither they nor their publishing companies will get any royalties? In fact all the income from sales of CompassionArt – the album that came out of this time together – will be channelled to charities in different parts of the world. The answer is a desire to see justice done. But equally, it was a desire to be obedient to God, who was calling each of them to become true worshippers and not just performers. Israel Houghton, one of the songwriters, captures the idea well for us:

'Working out that we can make a difference is often a gradual process, a slow growth away from thinking that our potential is limited towards the bright realisation that, with God, all

things are possible. There are no limits to what Christians can do
when it comes to fighting poverty. We can be a part of the solution,
part of the fix.
'And it starts with taking a look around and realising that poverty
and disease surrounds us but understanding that seeing the
world as it is does not negate us from doing something.'[1]

CompassionArt is not just about buying an album; it is an invitation
to consider a lifestyle change which will change the lives of others.

The big handover

I hope you have been able to feel a sense of ownership as well as a
sense of journey as we have considered 10.10.10. On that day prayer
will be at the very heart of our worship and action as we anticipate
100 million people across the world joining together to pray for the
poor and for justice. And then, to follow through, our goal is that
ten million people will make active promises of commitment to do
something practical about poverty.

But that is not enough and we cannot leave it there. As well as
taking part in prayer and practical action we also have the task
of advocating for and with the poor. Our prayers are not complete
without our commitment, and even our actions can become a safe
alternative to speaking up. And that's what I would like to ask you to
consider right now.

1,000 politicians reminded

Micah 2010 is an opportunity to encourage our leaders to remember
their promise to bring half a billion people out of extreme poverty
in our generation. Politicians need to hear that we care and that we
will hold them to account. They cannot push aside the Millennium
Development Goals agreed in 2000 as 'too hard' and we cannot let
the promise fail because of apathy or corruption.

The big handover of ten million handprints will remind our leaders
that we have only five years remaining to meet our promise. We
want to meet with at least 1,000 politicians in over 20 countries –
and your involvement will help us reach that target.

Ways to be involved in the Micah 2010 handover

Please make sure you add your hands count to the total global tally. Check whether there is a national count of the promise hands action in your country.

Invite your local politician to an event at church, eg for a meal or morning tea/coffee, at which you show how you are involved with the poor and make clear your support for the Millennium Development Goals. Present the handprints to your representative and ask him or her to pass on the hands and your requests to the appropriate government minister/secretary and to the prime minister/president. If the politician is agreeable pray for him or her and present the global prayer with the hands. You should be able to make an appointment to see your political representative at the national level if you live in a strong democracy. See the step-by-step guide at www.micah2010.org if you have never visited a politician before.

You may have a simple message for your political leader – 'Remember the Poor' – or you may have a message based on research done by the Micah Challenge campaign in your country. The more specific the message is, the more impact it will have. So check with Micah Challenge about issues and solutions in your country.

Join with other churches/groups in your area and visit your political representative together. This will show that there is strong support for action on poverty and will demonstrate that Christians are speaking with one voice. If you are not able to make contact with your local politician, send your handprints to the Micah Challenge office so that it can arrange a handover with an appropriate minister and talk about the two or three asks of the national campaign. These meetings will take place in the month following 10.10.10, so please pray for a positive outcome and tangible commitment.

Take photos and involve the media, eg your local paper or radio station. You can find a sample media release at www.micah2010.org

Remember to tell your church about the results of Micah 2010 in your country and around the world. You can register for news at www.micah2010.org

Working it out

Once again take some time to ask:

- How might this work in your church?

- Are there any aspects of this which look particularly difficult – or even unwise – in your context?

- How much would this kind of advocacy change you as a Christian witness?

- If we are effective in our witness, how might we measure the difference we make?

What is that one thing?

Our time with Micah has taken us to the heart of his message and the heart of God for the poor. As we have seen, humility is the foundation for any and all of our involvement. Mercy is our heart response to injustice. It is caught more than taught, so give God space to draw alongside you in making mercy real. Justice is our commitment to deal with injustice. In one sense if we are walking in humility and overflowing with mercy we can't help seeing righteousness responding to wrong.

So, with that in mind, what is that 'one thing' God is asking you to consider doing about injustice?

 FREE SONG DOWNLOAD
Visit www.micah2010.org to download Martin Smith's song 'You Have Shown Us'.

Note

[1]Israel Houghton in *The Art of Compassion*, Compassion Art (Hodder & Stoughton (UK), Faith Words (US), 2009). Used by permission.

Resources

Websites

Relief and development organisations

www.bread.org
www.christianaid.org.uk
www.compassion.com
www.eficor.org
www.fh.org
www.micahnetwork.org
www.progressio.org.uk
www.samaritanspurse.org
www.tearfund.org
www.ubs-goodsamaritan.org
www.worldrelief.org
www.worldvision.org

Denominational relief and development

www.adra.org
www.bwanet.org
www.caritas.org
www.convoyofhope.org
www.crwrc.org
www.interanglicanaid.org
www.lwr.org
www.mrdf.org.uk
www.salvationarmy.org
www.umc.org
www.worldevangelicals.org

Microfinance and microcredit

www.fivetalents.org
www.hopeinternational.org
www.opportunity.org

Creative involvement and campaigns

www.compassionart.tv
www.globalpovertyproject.com
www.i-heart.org
www.integralmission.net

www.micahchallenge.org
www.micah2010.org
www.one.org
www.toughstuffonline.org
www.traidcraft.co.uk

Justice organisations and campaigns

www.ijm.org
www.jubileedebtcampaign.org.uk
www.sojo.net
www.speak.org.uk
www.stopthetraffik.org
www.thea21campaign.org
www.tjm.org.uk

Books and other resources

The Art of Compassion, CompassionArt (London: Hodder & Stoughton, 2009).
CompassionArt – the album (CompassionArt).

Alkire, Sabina and Newell, Edmund, *What Can One Person Do? Faith to Heal a Broken World* (London: Darton, Longman and Todd, 2005).

Chester, Tim, ed., *Justice, Mercy and Humility, Integral Mission and the Poor* (Milton Keynes: Authentic, 2002).

Haugen, Gary, *Good News About Injustice* (Nottingham: IVP, 1999).

Hoek, Marijke and Thacker, Justin, *Micah's Challenge: The Church's Responsibility to the Global Poor* (Milton Keynes: Paternoster, 2008).

Myers, Bryant L., *Walking With the Poor* (London: Orbis Books, 1999).

Stearns, Richard, *The Hole In Our Gospel: What Does God Expect of Us?* (Nashville: Thomas Nelson, 2009).

Tearfund and Livability, *Just People? Equipping churches to respond to local and global poverty* – six-week interactive course with DVD (www.communitymission.org.uk)

Wallis, Jim, *Seven Ways to Change the World* (Oxford: Lion Publishing, 2009).

National Distributors

UK: (and countries not listed below)
CWR, Waverley Abbey House, Waverley Lane, Farnham, Surrey GU9 8EP.
Tel: (01252) 784700 Outside UK (44) 1252 784700 Email: mail@cwr.org.uk

AUSTRALIA: KI Entertainment, Unit 21 317-321 Woodpark Road, Smithfield, New South Wales 2164. Tel: 1 800 850 777 Fax: 02 9604 3699 Email: sales@kientertainment.com.au

CANADA: David C Cook Distribution Canada, PO Box 98, 55 Woodslee Avenue, Paris, Ontario N3L 3E5. Tel: 1800 263 2664 Email: swansons@cook.ca

GHANA: Challenge Enterprises of Ghana, PO Box 5723, Accra. Tel: (021) 222437/223249 Fax: (021) 226227 Email: ceg@africaonline.com.gh

HONG KONG: Cross Communications Ltd, 1/F, 562A Nathan Road, Kowloon.
Tel: 2780 1188 Fax: 2770 6229 Email: cross@crosshk.com

INDIA: Crystal Communications, 10-3-18/4/1, East Marredpalli, Secunderabad – 500026, Andhra Pradesh. Tel/Fax: (040) 27737145 Email: crystal_edwj@rediffmail.com

KENYA: Keswick Books and Gifts Ltd, PO Box 10242-00400, Nairobi.
Tel: (254) 20 312639/3870125 Email: keswick@swiftkenya.com

MALAYSIA: Canaanland, No. 25 Jalan PJU 1A/41B, NZX Commercial Centre, Ara Jaya, 47301 Petaling Jaya, Selangor. Tel: (03) 7885 0540/1/2 Fax: (03) 7885 0545 Email: info@canaanland.com.my

Salvation Book Centre (M) Sdn Bhd, 23 Jalan SS 2/64, 47300 Petaling Jaya, Selangor.
Tel: (03) 78766411/78766797 Fax: (03) 78757066/78756360
Email: info@salvationbookcentre.com

NEW ZEALAND: KI Entertainment, Unit 21 317-321 Woodpark Road, Smithfield, New South Wales 2164, Australia. Tel: 0 800 850 777 Fax: +612 9604 3699
Email: sales@kientertainment.com.au

NIGERIA: FBFM, Helen Baugh House, 96 St Finbarr's College Road, Akoka, Lagos.
Tel: (01) 7747429/4700218/825775/827264 Email: fbfm@hyperia.com

PHILIPPINES: OMF Literature Inc, 776 Boni Avenue, Mandaluyong City.
Tel: (02) 531 2183 Fax: (02) 531 1960 Email: gloadlaon@omflit.com

SINGAPORE: Alby Commercial Enterprises Pte Ltd, 95 Kallang Avenue #04-00, AIS Industrial Building, 339420. Tel: (65) 629 27238 Fax: (65) 629 27235 Email: marketing@alby.com.sg

SOUTH AFRICA: Struik Christian Books, 80 MacKenzie Street, PO Box 1144, Cape Town 8000.
Tel: (021) 462 4360 Fax: (021) 461 3612 Email: info@struikchristianmedia.co.za

SRI LANKA: Christombu Publications (Pvt) Ltd, Bartleet House, 65 Braybrooke Place, Colombo 2.
Tel: (9411) 2421073/2447665 Email: dhanad@bartleet.com

USA: David C Cook Distribution Canada, PO Box 98, 55 Woodslee Avenue, Paris, Ontario N3L 3E5, Canada. Tel: 1800 263 2664 Email: swansons@cook.ca

CWR is a Registered Charity – Number 294387
CWR is a Limited Company registered in England – Registration Number 1990308

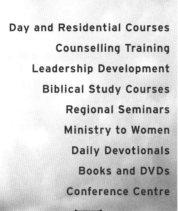

Day and Residential Courses
Counselling Training
Leadership Development
Biblical Study Courses
Regional Seminars
Ministry to Women
Daily Devotionals
Books and DVDs
Conference Centre

Trusted all Over the World

CWR HAS GAINED A WORLDWIDE reputation as a centre of excellence for Bible-based training and resources. From our headquarters at Waverley Abbey House, Farnham, England, we have been serving God's people for over 40 years with a vision to help apply God's Word to everyday life and relationships. The daily devotional *Every Day with Jesus* is read by nearly a million readers an issue in more than 150 countries, and our unique courses in biblical studies and pastoral care are respected all over the world. Waverley Abbey House provides a conference centre in a tranquil setting.

For free brochures on our seminars and courses, conference facilities, or a catalogue of CWR resources, please contact us at the following address:
CWR, Waverley Abbey House, Waverley Lane, Farnham, Surrey GU9 8EP, UK

Telephone: +44 (0)1252 784700
Email: mail@cwr.org.uk
Website: www.cwr.org.uk

CWR Applying God's Word
to everyday life and relationships

Devotional CD

Fifteen songs that join the dots between worship and justice. *You Have Shown Us* includes songs from Stuart Townend, Tim Hughes, Martin Smith, Brenton Brown, Lou Fellingham, Cathy Burton, Matt Redman, Chris Tomlin, Andy Bromley and Godfrey Birtill. All proceeds raised go to support Micah Challenge.

Available from Kingsway at www.kingsway.co.uk or from your local Christian bookshop.

£12.99 inc VAT
KMCD3130

Price correct at time of printing.

Be creatively compassionate

God has something to say about poverty, injustice, oppression and exploitation – and we need to hear it.

International speaker and Bible teacher Jeff Lucas takes us to India to help us answer the question 'How am I doing with my lifestyle?'

Based on Micah 6:8, *The Impossible Dream?* will enable you to creatively combine preaching the gospel with compassionate action on behalf of the weak and disadvantaged.

This resource pack includes:
• One DVD with six approximately 10-minute sessions
• One booklet with discussion starters, prayers and six weeks of daily Bible-reading notes.

EAN: 5027957001268
£18.99 inc VAT

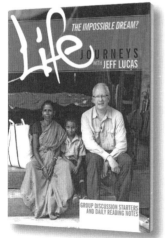

One booklet required for each group participant.
48 pages, 120x170mm
ISBN: 978-1-85345-531-5
£3.50 each

Prices correct at time of printing.

Life Issues Bible Study Guides

Our *Life Issues* series of Bible studies will help you think through important issues of contemporary life. Each study guide's four sessions include biblical teaching, discussion starters, personal application and reflection. Great for small-group or personal use!

Environment
Take a biblical look at environmental issues
ISBN: 978-1-85345-481-3

Forgiveness
Gain freedom from the past through the power of forgiveness
ISBN: 978-1-85345-446-2

Globalisation
Think through political, economic and environmental issues and consider the Church's role
ISBN: 978-1-85345-543-8

Money
Understand God's teaching about money and enjoy greater financial freedom
ISBN: 978-1-85345-513-1

Relationships
Discover the secret of fulfilling relationships
ISBN: 978-1-85345-447-9

Time
Create time for God, others and yourself
ISBN: 978-1-85345-517-9

Work
Turn your job into a blessing – for yourself and others
ISBN: 978-1-85345-480-6

£3.99 each
Price correct at time of printing.